THINK ENGLISH, SPEAK ENGLISH

HOW TO STOP PERFORMING MENTAL
GYMNASTICS EVERY TIME YOU SPEAK ENGLISH

DR JULIAN NORTHBROOK

CONTENTS

COMPLETE AUDIO VERSION OF THE BOOK

You can find an audio version of this book by following the URL in the "Resources" section (**note: as this is delivered via the Doing English "Learnistic" app, it's currently only available to people who have a smartphone**). I've done this because we learn best by repeating the same information multiple times in different formats. When you read, you learn in one way and when you listen, you learn in another. This ensures that you get the most benefit from what you learn here.

INTRODUCTION

Welcome to *Think English, Speak English: How to Stop Performing Mental Gymnastics Every Time You Speak English.*

I'm Dr Julian Northbrook, Second Language Acquisition researcher and founder of 'Doing English' – the place for 'high-level' English learners who want to add some "wow!" to their English-speaking ability.

Enough about me for now. There's a detailed "Who the hell is Julian Northbrook?" section at the back of this book if you care enough, including links to "Resources" and all that good stuff I've done to be found there.

You can find an audio version of this book by following the URL found, again, in the "Resources" section (**note: as this is delivered via the Doing English "Learnistic"**

app, it's currently only available to people who have a smartphone). I've done this because we learn best by repeating the same information multiple times in different formats. When you read, you learn in one way. When you listen, you learn in another. This ensures that you get the most benefit from what you learn here.

Starting with First Things First

This isn't a complete guide to learning and mastering English. If that's what you're looking for, you'd be **much** better off with my other core book, *Master English FAST – An Uncommon Guide to Speaking Extraordinary English.*

So, what is this book exactly?

Well, when I wrote *Master English FAST* (MEF) back in 2017, I was pretty short on space, and a lot had to be left out. I wasn't able to go as in-depth with some topics as I wanted to, and I had a lot of material left over. So eventually, I made the decision to make MEF the core guide, and then keep that extra stuff and release it later as this *"Quick 'n' Dirty English Learning Guides"* series of what you might call "other" English Learning topics. *Fearless Fluency* was focused on confidence when speaking English as a second language. *Secrets of Structured Learning* was focused on learning in a way that you never forget. *Awesome Accent* is about, you guessed it: accent... and the quality or "sound" of your speech when you speak.

This book, *Think English, Speak English* is focused on the topic of stopping translating in your head as you speak and overthinking everything – or what I like to call performing "mental gymnastics" every time you speak in English.

If you find yourself sounding slow and awkward because you're thinking of everything in your head in your native language, then this book is for you. Cutting out all that overthinking, and translation will help a lot. Aside from fluency, this'll also help you to sound more natural (because translated English is very rarely natural sounding). Before we move on, there are two things we need to note here:

First, I've purposely kept this book as short as I can. Why? Because, as I talked about extensively in my book *Secrets of Structured Learning*, learning "more" is very rarely the answer to getting *good*. We learn much, much better when we internalise and really use a smaller number of important concepts. I mention this because sometimes people feel disappointed because they haven't got "a lot" for their money... but this is stupid in the extreme because it's the value of the CONTENT that you learn that's important. Not the raw number of words.

Second, many (though certainly not all) of the examples used in this book come from Japanese because that's the language I know best other than English – but don't worry. Everything we talk about here is universal.

1. WHAT LANGUAGE DO YOU THINK IN?

WHEN YOU SPEAK ENGLISH, what language do you think in? Is it English?

Or is it your native language?

If you're reading this book, chances are you think in your native language... even when you're speaking English. And you know that's a problem.

It's a big problem, in fact.

While you are "thinking" in the wrong language, you will never speak fluently or naturally because that other language (probably your first language, though there are exceptions) will always get in the way.

One of my coaching clients asked me:

"How can I stop thinking in my native language and translating everything I want to say in English?"

And indeed, this is one of the most common questions I get in the weekly group coaching calls I do for my clients (more on that at the back of this book, if you're interested). Hence, it's the topic of this short book.

The first thing you've got to understand is, translating in your head is a habit. And it's a habit that can be hard to break for some people, not so much for others. But regardless, **it's a habit that you have created**. And the more you keep doing the wrong things (for example, are you studying grammar rules and memorising lists of words trying to improve your naturalness and fluency?) the stronger that habit will become, and the harder it's going to be to break.

And yes, I know that's frustrating.

It took you years to learn English... but you're still not getting the results you want. When you speak, the words don't come easily. You feel slow and awkward. You're thinking of everything in your first language, translating it into English and it doesn't feel good.

Well, I've got good news, and I've got bad news for you:

the good news is that – as I just said – this problem can be fixed with little time and effort.

The bad news is, your bad 'translation habits' are – as I've also just said – a hundred per cent a result of the way you learned English. So, to truly start thinking in English, you may need to unlearn some of what you know about improving your English (which, of course, is wrong anyway – because if what you knew wasn't wrong, you wouldn't be here).

2. THE UNFAIR THINKING ADVANTAGE

NOW AT THIS POINT, I've got a bit of a confession to make personally, I never had any problems with thinking in the wrong language when speaking my second language. You could say that I had an "unfair thinking advantage". I speak English as my first language and Japanese as my second language. I think in the language I'm speaking in. I have always done this, even right from the beginning of learning Japanese. There are good reasons for this to do with how I learned the language and how I set up my day-to-day learning routine. I also had a huge advantage over most people learning English. Simply put, I was a *terrible* student at school. I completely refused to study the second language I was told to learn (French), and failed it. And this sounds bad – and I guess it kind of is – but it meant that when I started Japanese, I had to start from zero and I had no preconceived ideas about how I should learn it. No assumptions. No bad habits.

Most people have had years of school telling them they have to study grammar, combine those rules with words, and carefully think about what they say in order to "create" the sentences in their mind (accurately of course – otherwise your teacher will punish you with bad grades). I didn't know this. So, I never did it. More on that in a little while, though, because we're getting ahead of ourselves once again.

First, why is thinking in the wrong language even a problem?

Why does translating in your head as you speak slow you down so much and make your English awkward sounding?

The first step to answering these questions is understanding what fluency is, and we need to think about why you aren't fluent already.

3. WHY YOU AREN'T FLUENT

THIS SHOULD BE OBVIOUS BUT, thinking in a different language to the one you're speaking will hamper fluency. Badly.

Let's consider one of my clients, Mei (pseudonym), as an example. She's an excellent example of someone who had a lot of trouble with thinking in her first language whilst trying to speak English and subsequently translating everything in her head as she went (note the past tense; we have long since fixed these problems for her and now she speaks with ease and grace).

When we first met, she was constantly performing mental gymnastics when she spoke English. So much so, that it's amazing she could speak at all. To say the simplest of sentences in English, first, she thought of what she wanted to say in Japanese (her first language) and then she planned it out in her head, translating the individual words. Next, she would stick those words together using the grammar rules she'd learned at school. Finally, she'd start, slowly, but surely to say the sentence – slowly, carefully, one word at a time, all while trying to hold the sentence she'd just created in memory.

Not exactly the best way to speak a language. If all you need to do is ask the way to the train station or order a coffee, it might be okay – but a fluent conversation is impossible.

Unsurprisingly, Mei got tired speaking in English very quickly. Of course, she did! Just think how much was going on in her brain as she tried to speak! Also, unsurprisingly, she was quite frustrating to talk to in English. It took her forever to get out a single sentence. Not only that, but it always sounded awkward and convoluted – more like Japanese said in English words rather than actual English.

A question on the Q&A site, Quora, asked if native English speakers enjoyed speaking with non-natives. The vast majority of answers to this question were positive, BUT only when the person was able to keep the conversation flowing. Well, if you're currently speaking like my client Mei was, you're not keeping the conversation flowing... quite the opposite. So don't be surprised if people don't enjoy talking to you. Harsh, I know, but still true.

The truth is, it's very tiring to listen to disfluent English – especially if your English is also unnatural sounding. And by this, I mean "grammatical" but totally un-nativelike in the way you've said it. You see, although, yes, it is grammatical... being unnatural in this way forces the listener to work really hard to understand you because the things you say aren't expected (i.e., they're not predictable like natural sounding expressions are). And if you're translating from your first language, well you can pretty much just say goodbye to naturalness.

4. GOODBYE, NATURALNESS!

SOMETHING YOU'VE TRANSLATED in your head from your native language to English will never ever sound natural. After all, no two languages are the same. Unless you are extremely proficient in both languages and understand perfectly the way speakers of those two languages think (their culture – more on that later), it's very hard to translate well.

You've probably seen films or TV programmes with subtitles that sound odd. Dubbing tends to be even worse – it is English (or whatever language the film has been dubbed into), but it doesn't sound like normal, natural English.

It's quite easy to spot English that has been translated from Japanese, for example, because it reflects a

Japanese way of thinking and of expressing things. Not an English way of thinking or expressing things.

As I said, translating things naturally is hard even for translators or interpreters; so, it's going to be next to impossible for you to do it in your head on the fly while speaking. Things often get mixed up and mistranslated – we suffer terribly from something that language scientists call "Negative Transfer". In fact, this is why people who are suddenly told by their boss, for example, "Hey, you speak English – translate this!" struggle so much: translation is a skill in and of itself, separate to simply knowing your languages.

Once upon a time, a teacher at a school where I worked said to me, *"I'm so busy I'd like to borrow a cat's hand!"* To her, it seemed to be the most natural, obvious thing in the world to say. But I had no idea what she meant at the time. Now, I know that this was a direct translation of the idiom: *"nook no te wo kittenhood isogashii"* – literally: "I would even borrow a cat's hand, I'm so busy". This is an idiom that doesn't exist in English. So, translating it into English doesn't make any sense whatsoever. Similarly, I read a great story about an exchange student in France. She'd eaten a lot of food, and said to her host family, *"Je sues plein!"* – *"I am full"*. Only, in French *"I am full"* is an idiom that means "I'm pregnant" (cue much-amused laughter).

We've all made mistakes like this, of course. I know I certainly have. In a Japanese tavern (an *Izakaya*) I once asked for chicken hearts – a type of chicken skewer kebab that's not only popular there but extremely delicious. Written in English, this might not sound so strange to you: until you realise that the word "heart" actually has two meanings. It can mean 'heart' as in the emotion; *"I love you with all my heart"* – something akin to a person's *soul*. This is *"kokoro"* in Japanese. The other meaning – the thing inside your body, the actual organ – in Japanese is *"shinzo"*. The two things are very distinct and very separate. So, as you can imagine, I got some quite strange looks asking for a *"Chicken's kokoro, please"* ... a chicken's *soul* on a kebab skewer.

Now, this said, (and this is a slight digression and invalidates my point slightly, but it's also a good learning point... so whatever) my now ex-wife used to laugh at me all the time about this incident to the extent where if I ever laughed at her English for any reason, she came back with, "TORI NO KOKORO!". Of course, it was all meant in good humour. But then a reader of an early draft of this very book emailed me to say that, in Kansai (a different part of Japan from where I lived), people actually do call this particular delicacy *tori no kokoro*. So, the mistake wasn't as strange and amusing as it sounded... or at least, it wouldn't, if I had lived in a totally different part of Japan!

5.   THE TRANSLATION MISTAKES
YOU DON'T KNOW YOU MAKE

THESE KINDS of mistakes are fairly obvious, and as long as you know that an idiom, for example, does or doesn't exist in English or in your first language, you're unlikely to make this mistake. But "negative transfer" also happens on a much deeper, much trickier level and there are translation mistakes that you make that you don't even know you make.

A fantastic example of this, once again from Japanese, are the words "this" and "that":

"kore" – *This.*

"sore" – *That.*

"are" – ... *That over there.*

"*Kore*" refers to something close to the speaker; "*sore*" refers to something close to the person you're talking to; and "*are*" refers to an object that is neither close to the speaker nor to the listener. First, Japanese has an extra word – "*are*" (which English kind of has, but as a phrase – "that over there").

This is already quite confusing. But to make matters worse, the way Japanese people *think* about the relationship between a person and the position of an object is very different to an English speaker. For example, imagine you're sitting in front of the TV, watching a cooking show. The presenter whips up some delicious-looking food. In English, you'd look at the TV and say: "*That looks amazing!*" ... but not so in Japanese. Rather, you'd have to say: "*kore wa oishiso!*" – "This looks amazing!" It's a very subtle difference, but in English "this" sounds just as weird as "that" sounds in Japanese.

This kind of "negative transfer" can be very hard to overcome because the incorrect "that" always sounds more natural to a native-English speaker.

Even after living in Japan and speaking the language for something like 14 years, "*kore wa oishiso*" (this) sounds strange as hell to me, and unnatural when referring to something on the TV. It just doesn't seem that it's a "this" kind of situation.

It sounds strange and unnatural to me to the extent where I still – even now – doubt that it's correct. Writing this book, I checked it several times just to be sure.

"Surely that can't be right...," my brain says.

The best, and probably only way to get over this problem and stop making mistakes, is to forget about the actual words and learn the phrase as a chunk – as a single unit of language – that can be used automatically in the right situation. And indeed – this is how native speakers use their language.

I'll talk a lot more about this in a bit, because it's a super important part of the solution to this "mental gymnastics" problem.

First, though, we still need to understand a couple of core concepts.

Specifically, why this translation happens.

6. SO WHY ARE YOU STUCK TRANSLATING IN YOUR HEAD?

AN INTERESTING QUESTION, right?

Simply put, it all comes down to a combination of your attitude, your proficiency, and the way you learned English in the first place. This also includes the kind of language you learned and subsequent bad habits you've formed since. Oh, and something Language Scientists call "Activation" – which I'll talk about in detail in a moment.

Right away, you'll see, that mental gymnastics don't happen for any single, simple reason. It's complex.

This complexity is why this habit is hard to break. And why a lot of the over-simplistic advice floating around on the internet doesn't really work.

"Just think in English!" people say.

Riiiiight!

Not like you'd never thought of that...

Telling someone to "just start thinking in English" is like telling someone with clinical depression to "just cheer up" ... it sounds kind of logical, but only if you've got no fucking idea what you're actually talking about or dealing with (meaning it's crap advice and you should keep your mouth shut... but I digress).

But don't worry, the habit can be broken. And all habits can be broken.

7. HOW YOU BECAME A MENTAL GYMNAST

LET'S go back to what I said about Mei, my coaching girl. She went to the top high school in Japan and graduated with top grades in everything (including English). And herein lies the problem – *she did a great job of learning English at school.*

Only the English she was taught at school, was, well, not exactly the sort of thing you find useful in the real world. She was taught English in basically the same way as you're taught maths – with the specific goal of solving problems, passing entrance exams, and getting great grades. Both of which were focused on accuracy and translating from Japanese into English and vice-versa. The result was that she essentially spent years *practising* these mental gymnastics. She learned how to analyse sentences and translate them back-and-forth between two languages without ever having to produce language in the way we naturally speak. Her translation problem was, then, a learned condition: practised in the classroom, and re-enforced by feedback based purely on accuracy – i.e., she was punished for mistakes and praised for grammatical accuracy, regardless of fluency or naturalness (because grammatical English and 'natural' English are totally not the same thing).

Compare this with the way I learned Japanese. Right from the start, I was focused on speaking and communicating the meaning in the language. When I was first working in Japan as an English teacher, nobody cared about how crap my Japanese was as long as they could get the meaning. We had a job to do, and I HAD to get it done, regardless of the mistakes that I made. But if I took a long time making a sentence… I was punished with a look of extreme impatience. So right from the start I got used to speaking fast and thinking directly in Japanese – even if that meant I wasn't as accurate as I could have been.

Simply put, you get good at what you do. And if what you do is convoluted mental gymnastics, well, that's what you will get good at.

It's not just *how* you learn, though. Because *what* you learn is very important – and this is what I'll talk about next before turning to the equally important topic of how to "activate" what you've learnt.

8. HOW NATIVE SPEAKERS SPEAK

MEI LEARNED the wrong way to speak fluent English (i.e., the method). But the kind of English she learned made her problem much worse, too. She learned grammar rules and vocabulary. And then she tried to combine those in her head as she spoke. But she learned very little in the way of 'chunks' of language – and the ones that she did learn weren't the kind that she needed for real life, anyway.

So, ask yourself, why can native speakers speak so fluently?

Why can they understand others so easily?

Why do even very advanced English learners often sound "different" to native speakers?

And why do natives pronounce language like they do?

The answer to all these questions is:

CHUNKING.

We used to think that native speakers used vocabulary and grammar rules to create sentences. But this never really made sense. Native speakers speak too fluently, using very predictable patterns of language (i.e., they sound 'natural'). For someone learning English, something like "make a picture" and "take a picture" might seem the same. They mean the same thing, after all. They're both grammatical. So why do us natives only say, "take a picture"?

Well, for a native speaker, these two expressions are completely different. It's all about chunking. To a native speaker, "take a picture" is a chunk, a high frequency, a highly probable block of English – a single unit of language, like one single word that is likely to be used and that it's processed in the brain as such. There's a lot of argument in academic research about exactly how this happens, but it doesn't really matter. What matters is how a native speaker says and understands the phrase "take a picture". But something like "make a picture" is not a chunk – or at least not in the sense of a high frequency, highly probable piece of English. It has to be made using the grammar rule "verb + noun phrase [determiner + noun]", combined with the individual words (make, a, picture). And as a result, it takes more processing power to say and to understand. It has to be computed in a way that "take a picture" never has to be. And it's also a very unlikely combination. The chunk "take a picture", however, is extremely common in English; "make a picture" is not.

What this means for you is that **good chunking skills are essential**. You need to start seeing English as CHUNKS. Not individual words. But chunks of English. Things like, "how's it going", "I didn't know what to say" (used when something seems unbelievable and you're lost for words) or idioms such as, "A little bird tells me..." (used when you want to say you've heard something from someone, but don't want to say who) are all very obvious chunks and are very easy to spot. But things like, "a lot of the", "in the middle of the" or, "on the other hand" are all chunks, too.

Native speakers store huge numbers of these chunks in long-term memory. And when they speak, instead of using grammar rules and words they just pull these ready-made, complete chunks out of long-term memory and use them as is.

Again, for those interested in the science behind this, there is a lot of argument about exactly how all this happens. It could be that the brain literally stores chunks as single word-like units in memory. Or it could be that the brain maps these chunks to statistical information – kind of like automatic "language habits" (which is, incidentally, the theory my own lab-research tends to support and what I tend to believe more likely...do a Google Scholar search for "Julian Northbrook" if you're interested in this). Honestly, unless you're going to get into the research side of things, though, it doesn't matter how it happens. The result is the same regardless: chunks of English are produced and understood automatically, without needing complicated (not to mention exhausting) grammar-processing.

You don't really need more words.

In reality, very few people need to learn more vocabulary.

You only think you do.

But you're wrong.

See, it's not that you don't know "enough" words, but rather, you're simply combining the words they already have badly – they don't know chunks, and that's what causes you to speak slowly and awkwardly. Yes, knowing more words is great. But just understand that learning more words won't do much to fix your fluency problems if you're not learning in, and speaking in, chunks of English instead of grammar and words.

This is a slight digression, but several years ago I did a research project of Japanese secondary school English textbooks. I analysed all the words in the textbooks, and they were actually okay, meaning they were all fairly common words used in everyday situations. But when we analysed the conversations, we found that the large chunks these words were used in were totally different to the ones native speakers would use in a real-life conversation. In fact, they were so different that you could almost consider the language taught in the textbooks to be a *new* language – a language made from English words and grammar rules, **but not actually English**. The point is, what is important is not how many words you know... but your knowledge of how they are combined. The language you learn matters. So do the materials you use.

Chunks will help you speak fluently and naturally like native speakers do. But there's also another reason why you need to see language as chunks – unlike words, chunks are hard to translate. Which means less "activation" of your first language.

What does that mean exactly?

Well, let's think about how we can flip the thinking-switch of "activation" from your first language to English, when you're speaking English...

9. TIME TO FLIP THE THINKING-SWITCH

THE CONCEPT OF "ACTIVATION" is a technical one that you don't need to know beyond what it actually is... again; we're not learning to be language scientists here. We just want to speak better English. But it's a very important part of fluency, so it's well worth discussing here in practical terms.

Garcia, one of my *League of Extraordinary English Speakers* members (the MEFA graduate programme – see "implementation course" at the end of this book) sent a message to the discussion group saying:

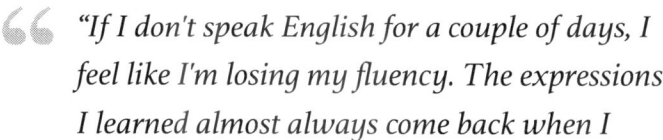 *"If I don't speak English for a couple of days, I feel like I'm losing my fluency. The expressions I learned almost always come back when I*

speak more. However, it takes some time to wake them up."

And then he went on to say:

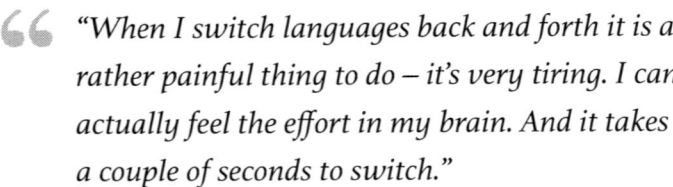

"When I switch languages back and forth it is a rather painful thing to do – it's very tiring. I can actually feel the effort in my brain. And it takes a couple of seconds to switch."

There are some very important insights in this.

Let's start with the first part because it's the easiest (and indeed the most important).

First:

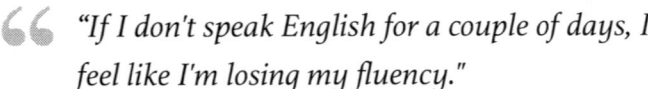

"If I don't speak English for a couple of days, I feel like I'm losing my fluency."

This feeling of "losing fluency" comes from the way the brain controls the different languages it has. If you know two languages (or more) those languages are *always* active in your brain. They're always switched on. Always. Not necessarily equally – coming to that in a second – but they are always switched on.

Now, imagine your first language is French, but you also know English. You see a book lying on the table. This is what happens in your brain:

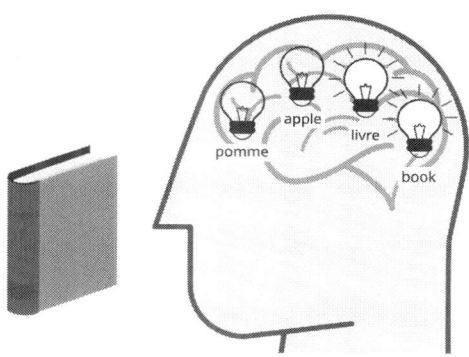

In your mind, the word "livre" will become activated. BUT – and this is important – so will the English word "book". Obviously, the words "apple" and "pomme" are going to stay inactive because they're irrelevant to the current situation. (The person in the picture isn't looking at an apple, after all.)

If I took the book away, however, and replaced it with an apple then we'd get the opposite effect:

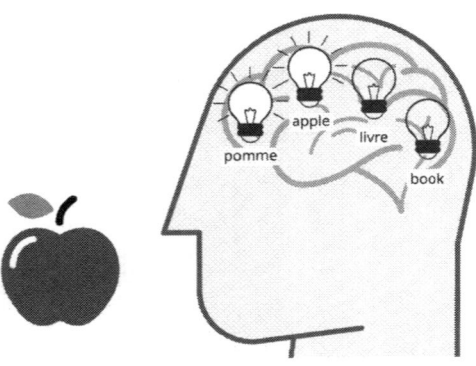

The words "livre" and "book" just switch off and the French and English words for apple, "apple" and "pomme" would light up.

This is a massive oversimplification. Language Science, or "Psycholinguistics", which is a part of what I did in my Ph.D. and Masters, is a very complicated science. But I'm just trying to give you the idea here.

Now, for comprehension, this isn't much of a problem. Both "book" and the French word "livre" are attached to the same meaning, after all. So whichever route your brain takes... comprehension occurs. You understand what the thing is. The only difference is the language that you _think_ of it in.

But what about speaking?

Well, that's a little different. You don't want to be speaking English and mistakenly say: *"Could you pass me that livre?"* (and if you are French speaking English, you may well have done something just like this – and now you know why it happens). But in this situation, every time you want to say "book", your brain chooses between two active words – "book" and "livre". This creates competition – both alternatives **WANT** to be chosen... *and so they fight*. The harder it is for one side to win out against the other, the longer speaking will take. Incidentally, the constant fighting between languages strengthens your mental muscle (cognitive control) which is why bilinguals tend to be more creative, and have better metalinguistic skills, keep a sharp mind in old age... and a whole host of other benefits (but more on that another time).

The point is, you are constantly selecting between alternative languages. The brain does an amazing job of this. People rarely make mistakes (though, as I mentioned a second ago, they occasionally do – and you've probably had this experience of saying a word in the wrong language; I know I certainly have). But of course... **all this fighting uses a lot of the brain's energy.** So, to combat this, the brain has a kind of suppression mechanism. This is where "activation" comes in.

Look at the illustrations above again.

Do you notice something strange about them?

Right.

In those illustrations, the English and French lightbulbs are equally bright (i.e., they are equally "active"). But unless you're a simultaneous interpreter or something like that, this is very rarely going to happen. If French is your first language, it's going to have a lot more strength simply because it's your first language.

If you've been speaking French all day, reading French, listening to French on the radio, for example, and everybody around you is speaking French... well, French is going to be REALLY active in your brain. So, those little lightbulbs are not going to be equally lit up. They'll look more like this:

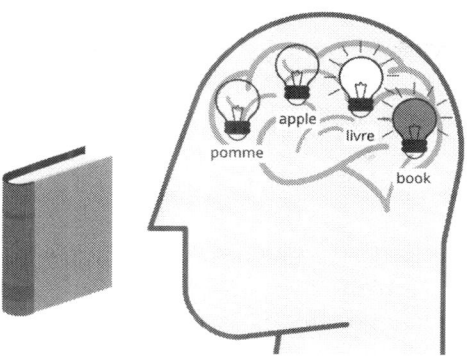

The French word "livre" is really bright and the word "book" is still lit up, but quite dull in comparison. Or to put it another way, the English word is weak compared to French. To put it another way, English has a low "activation" in comparison. It's weak and half asleep. Not completely (because it *never* completely switches off). But English doesn't stand a chance in comparison to French in this situation. When these two words fight it out, the French equivalent is going to win very quickly. And it's pretty unlikely we're going to select the wrong word, or experience interference from our English (and yes – even if French is your first language, you can, and will, experience interference from your second language, i.e., English, as your proficiency increases, but once again I digress).

Now, imagine you're in your office, and you've been speaking English all day long, and everything around you are now in English:

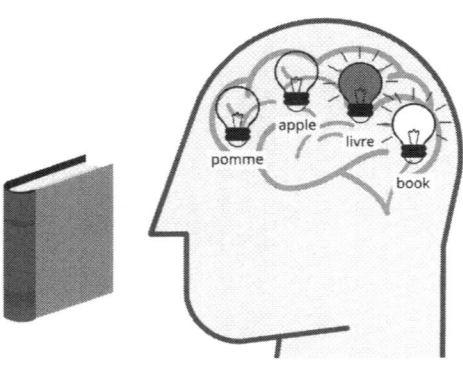

What the illustration above shows is that we now have the exact opposite thing going on. Even though you're looking at the same book, and your first language is still French... the French equivalent, "livre", is now somewhat dull in comparison to the English version. Which is lit up like a Christmas tree light due to its high level of "activation".

Clearly in this situation, it's English that is going to win out much easier because **there's far less competition from French** (which is now fairly inactive and half asleep).

Again, I need to make it clear that this is a massive oversimplification. This isn't supposed to be an academic textbook, though. So if you can get the basic idea of what "activation" is and understand why it happens like this... that's enough.

One more thing: we don't primarily speak in individual words like this, either. So, the illustrations that I've made are not only grossly oversimplified but, in a way, they're actually quite inaccurate. But again, there's a point that I'm trying to make, and as long as you understand the concept, that's fine. But I'm just pointing this out because moving from individual words to thinking in chunks is, as I've already said, a very important part for breaking the 'mental gymnastics' habit.

So, now we know what "activation" is, and we also know that we need to keep our English bright and awake if we don't want to be slow, sluggish, and constantly translate everything.

The next question is, how do you keep your English awake and active?

10. KEEP YOUR ENGLISH BUZZED

LIKE MOST PEOPLE in this world, the first thing I do when I wake up in the morning is reach for the coffee pot. Five minutes later, that sluggish, half-asleep, brain-won't-work feeling has melted away, leaving instead a pleasant caffeine-buzz (and let's be honest, a much, much more cheerful Julian, too... I am NOT good with people before coffee).

Now, unfortunately, you can't just give your English a double shot of espresso.

Not literally, anyway. It would be nice if you could. But we can do something very similar.

There are several factors that contribute to "activation" ... and I'm not going to discuss all of them here because we just don't have space (and some of them are far too technical and just not relevant to this discussion). But the important ones that you need to know about are:

1.Quantity of exposure to English.

2.Recency of exposure to English.

Think of the quantity of exposure as being like a set of those old-fashioned kitchen scales. On one side is English, and on the other side is your native language. The more English you pile on, the more the balance falls to the "English" side. Start using your first language... and the scales begin to tip the other way.

This is less like a quick-caffeine buzz, and more like eating too much junk food every day. You don't instantly get fat, but over time those pounds are going to pile on until you change your eating habits... and then your weight creeps back down again. The only difference here is not only that junk food's delicious, but it is actually pretty healthy for your English too – because you WANT to pile on the English pounds until it reaches heavy-weight sumo-wrestler proportions. Because that's the only way it's going to realistically stand a chance for fighting against your first language... which has been pigging out since you were born and now resembles Jabba the Hutt.

The average wrestler apparently eats around 20,000 calories a day, which is pretty incredible when you consider the typical male consumes around 2,500 calories a day.

But that wouldn't help them get as big as they do if they only ate that much once a week. Hell no. These guys eat that much every single bloody day.

Remember: if you totally stop eating, your body starts to burn off the calories and your weight is reduced. And this is exactly the same for your English, though it happens much faster.

Because of this, how recently you used a given language is also very important.

Here's another good analogy for this:

When I was a kid, I had a "dynamo light" on my bike.

Have you seen these?

They're a kind of a bicycle light that has a tiny built-in generator. As you pedal, you pump up the light with power. The faster you pedal, the brighter the light gets. But when you stop, the light starts to slowly fade as the built-up energy disappears.

Language is similar.

The more you use your English, the more it'll pump up your English "light". But when you stop... the built-up energy will quickly fade. And you can probably see the parallels here with the "eating a lot of food, get fat; stop eating, lose weight" analogy. It just happens here on a much faster scale. So because of this, your English is always going to be strongest <u>immediately</u> after using English.

So to keep your English strong, and to stop your native language from getting in the way, you need to use (and that can mean: hear, read, speak, study, learn, write – anything you <u>do</u> in English, 'using' doesn't just mean speaking, like people mistakenly think it does) English as much as you can... but also – and I believe this is more important – you need to use it as often as you can.

This is why I'm always telling people it's much better to spend 10 minutes a day learning English than two hours, once a week.

Yes, quantity matters.

But frequency is also super important, too.

Before we move on, one more quick thing to mention: switching languages is tiring, and the more active the language you're switching FROM the worse it'll be.

Do you remember what my *Extraordinary English Speakers* member I mentioned earlier, Garcia, said?

"Switching between languages is tiring."

This is why.

You can think of it as like going forward or reversing in a car. If the car is stationary, it doesn't take much to make it move forward or backwards. But if you're hurtling down the motorway at 100 miles an hour and then suddenly try to reverse, you're fighting against the forward momentum. Actually, I don't drive... so I can only imagine how much damage it would do to your car and it might be impossible for all I know... But the point is, if I spend an evening with my Japanese-speaking friends, I'm thinking only in Japanese, and as a result, English feels hard. That's because my Japanese "activation" is right up, and to switch to English, I've got to fight against the flow. Of course, if I'm not using Japanese at all, but rather, I'm speaking in English, the opposite happens. So naturally, if I'm using Japanese a lot and I want to keep it sharp, I want to keep my everyday environment as Japanese as possible. In truth, this is really just an example, I don't actually use Japanese at the moment and it's not a priority for me. However, that's fine; I know that if I ever need to, I can wake it up again whenever I want.

11. 5 WAYS TO TRAIN YOURSELF TO "THINK ENGLISH, SPEAK ENGLISH"

So, first, let me just reiterate that good news that I gave you towards the beginning of this book: if you suffer from the same kind of mental gymnastics as my client Mei did, then don't worry. It is relatively simple to fix. It doesn't mean that it's going to be easy, it also doesn't mean that it's not going to take some time and effort. But fixing the problem is relatively simple.

You've probably already noticed, but to a certain extent, this is one of those things where simply understanding *why* it happens is enough to kick-start the process of breaking the bad habit. You never improve what you don't notice, after all. And if you don't notice your bad translation habits, or indeed, even that they are indeed habits that **you've** created, they never get better.

Conversely, once you notice it, it's really quite easy to stop. There are, however, a couple of things you can do to speed up the process above and beyond simply noticing and being aware of the problem.

But before I give them to you, I need to just point out something very quickly: honestly, what I'm going to talk about in this section can be a little bit frustrating for me. Because it's not as simple as it sounds, and there are subtleties to what I'm talking about here. But people tend to just hear, "Simply think in English!" and get it quite wrong. I've already told you why that idea is just kind of quite stupid. It's like saying to a depressed person "just cheer up". Yeah, like it's going to be that fucking easy, like I never thought about that... It doesn't help, again, also as I've mentioned earlier in this book, that there is a TON of bullshit advice floating around on t'internet about this.

So don't just look at the ideas, believe you know what they're all about and then skip past them thinking that you know what I'm going to say. Because you probably don't. And it's not as simple as just saying, "practise thinking in English", it doesn't work like that. Again, there are important subtleties, and these are what makes these exercises work, or to put it another way, to use one of my favourite idioms, "the devil is in the details", and if you get the details wrong, well, it's not going to work.

In fact, I don't actually recommend you try to "practise" thinking at all.

That's the wrong way to think about this stuff.

Instead <u>train</u> yourself to just do it.

This might sound like this is the same thing, but it's not. When you "practise" thinking in English all you're doing is trying to force something to happen... and that's the wrong way to do it. Your brain will resist, and you'll likely just make more problems for yourself (i.e., more bad habits). Because, yeah, you want more of those. Not! But when you train yourself in the right kind of way, thinking in English just happens as a by-product.

To put it another way, you want to 'nudge' your brain towards thinking in English by encouraging it to do the things that it wants to do anyway... just in English. You don't want to try and force it. Again, nudging and encouraging, excellent. Forcing just ends in resistance.

1. *Engage Your Fantasies*

Something I've always done (and I think everyone does to an extent) is have fantasy conversations in my head. I can't help it. When I'm walking or if I'm out on my bike, or out running, I'm having conversations in my head all the time. Often, I'm problem-solving, discussing things I need to work out (say, in my business), but often I'm just fantasising about some totally random shit, like being a famous rock star on stage, singing in front of millions of people, which is kind of stupid because I've never wanted to be a rock star, and I can't sing...

But at a very early stage, these conversations switched from English to Japanese. This wasn't a conscious decision, but kind of like when you fantasise about, again, being a rock star on stage, singing the song you've got playing in your ears.

I remember when I was still in the UK (just before going to Japan) and I only knew some basic greetings in Japanese and how to count to ten, basically. It sounds stupid, but I'd be walking down the road fantasising about bumping into a cute Japanese girl and launching into conversation: "Hi! My name's Julian! One-two-three-four-five-six-seven-eight...!" The funny thing is, these stupid conversations were just as exciting as imagining myself as a famous rock star performing in front of millions of people… maybe I'm just strange? But this really helped me to speak Japanese from a very early stage, using only the language that I knew.

Even now when I speak Japanese, if there's a word that I don't know or if there's something I don't know how to say – I'm not thinking it in English. It's just like there's a blank hole in my head that needs to be filled. This is because I'm used to thinking in Japanese when I speak the language – not thinking in English when I speak Japanese.

The key point here, again, is to not force it.

Encourage your brain to fantasise in English by nudging it… but not by forcing it. With plenty of frequent exposure, along with regular studying and learning, you just automatically start to do this anyway.

But again, don't force it, because that would just be counterproductive.

The second thing you can, and should, do is to switch your inner dialogue to English, and this is obviously very closely related to the point that we've just talked about.

2. *Switch Your Inner Dialogue to English*

Another way to put this is that everything that you do in English, including "thinking", should be real.

If you're having conversations in English, have it because you're enjoying talking to a friend, building a relationship with that person, or getting a job done inside the office. Don't do it for "practise", which, if that's the only reason you're doing it, is totally pointless, and the wrong way to approach things.

Thinking in English is the same.

Make it real.

For example, if I'm at home, I'm not sitting around telling myself, "Oh my god I've got to think about something in Japanese!". But this is what people start to do when they start talking about 'practise thinking in English'. They sit, they're staring into space, trying to force themselves to think about something in English. Don't do it like that. Switch your inner dialogue instead. And what I mean by that is if I'm going to make coffee and the coffee isn't in the cupboard where I normally keep it (because let's face it, I tend to just stick shit randomly in the cupboards, and then can't remember where the hell I've put it), I might think to myself, "Where the fuck's the coffee...". And instead of just doing that in my first language, I want to nudge that towards my second language.

Again, the difference here is very subtle, but one's real, the other is not. Just sitting there practising how to think in English is not going help you at all. Switching that inner dialogue, nudging it towards English instead of your first language, that's a real thing, and it's something that you actually do anyway in your first language.

And again, I know I'm repeating myself here. But as I try to drill right into the brains of my coaching clients right from Week 1 of the implementation course (again, see the back of this book), doing "fake" things develops the wrong kind of habits, which is the same when it comes to "practising" thinking in English.

When you go to the supermarket, talk yourself through the whole process in English – everything you need to buy, where you'll find the baskets, what you want to say to the cute checkout girl or guy (whatever your preference). Search for the items you need in English. Again, this is something you probably do in your first language. We all do it. We all wander around the supermarket, thinking, "oh yeah I put the coffee somewhere, and now I can't find it, so I better buy some more", "Where is the coffee, it's just over there", "Oh wait a minute, I've skipped the first aisle", and "I need to get some carrots". We all do it in our first language, anyway, so just try to nudge that towards English.

Again, go back to the fantasising in English part. Fantasise about bumping into an English speaker and just chatting with them. Just like you might fantasise about asking that cute checkout girl or guy out on a date. Just like you would in your first language. But **don't force it, nudge it.** Keep it in English. If there are holes in your English... so be it. Don't worry about them. Just keep going with the fantasy. Remember: you get good at what you do. And so, in this kind of fantasy-thinking conversation situation, you only want to be doing it in English.

This works, but yeah, it's hard at first. Again, the key here is to keep it real, let it come over time and don't force it.

The third thing that you can, and definitely should be doing, is focusing on chunks.

3. Focus on Chunks

We've talked a lot about chunks already, but let's talk about them some more.

As I said, native speakers don't speak by combining grammar rules and words (not most of the time, anyway). They speak using prefabricated chunks of language stored in long-term memory.

This by itself will help a great deal with fluency, because the less work your brain must do, the better. But also, as I already said, chunks don't need any complicated translation, and often, they can't be translated word-for-word anyway, or at least not easily.

When I was writing an early version of this book (several years ago now – what you're reading has been updated), my now ex-wife was sitting on a chair near me, and she suddenly said; "Aa! Sentaku wo hosanakucha!"

She forgot to hang out the washing.

If you're in the bad habit of translating, you'd end up doing something like this: "'sentaku' equals 'washing', and 'hosu' is... er... 'dry?' ... 'hang?', 'nakucha' is 'got to' so we have 'washing hang got to' ... 'got to hang the washing'" ... which clearly is over-complicated. But ONLY because you're thinking of it as individual words. If you just learned this as a complete unit in the first place, "I've got to hang out the washing", there is no mental gymnastics.

So, learn in chunks first.

Then over time, if we constantly associate the act of hanging out the washing with the phrase or with the chunk "hang out the washing" by thinking it in English, it'll become automatic; and you won't translate it anymore.

4. Focus on Overall Meaning and Concepts

This is closely related to the previous point about seeing English as a system of chunks but it's worth listing this separately.

A common trait of people who struggle with English is that they tend to over-analyse everything about the language they see.

Close analytical study can be very useful to notice things about English.

Yes.

It can.

And this is a really powerful way to learn and deepen your knowledge of English. And indeed, I do talk about this extensively in my main book, *Master English Fast*. But don't get into the habit of doing it all the time. There's a time for study, and there's a time for doing, and the 'doing time' is not the time for analysing.

Take samples of language – conversations, for example – and learn them as is. One of the benefits of being an *Extraordinary English Speakers* member is that you get weekly "episodes" (i.e., lessons) to study from me. I take a conversational story (based on a real-life sample of language) that we collect and then optimise it into a short, easy-to-use written story, and then teach all the chunks, phrases and expressions, and everything that appears in it. But I almost never discuss individual words in the lessons, or break-down the larger blocks of language. I focus on the overall meaning – *units of meaning*. This is important because I don't want you to develop a translation habit. I want you to focus on the chunks and the overall meaning in a way that comprehension and understanding and using just happens in your mind, as is.

The truth is many of the things native speakers say aren't grammatical anyway. "Thanks very much" for example is not a grammatical expression in English, but every native speaker says it all the time, and we don't think of it as strange or weird because it's "ungrammatical". Being "grammatical" doesn't explain native speaker language. And if you try to analyse this and work out why is it "thanks very much" even though that's not grammatical, well... this is just going to be counterproductive because you'll just get confused and doubt yourself. Everything will look weird and crazy. So forget about analysing it and just try to pick up all the individual little parts and instead, just take these common phrases and expressions (these high frequency chunks of English) that people use at face value, and just use them yourself, as is, without trying to completely pick them apart.

5. More Relaxed Exposure to English, More Often

Focused, intensive study of English – that is daily study – is important for constant growth. Yes, but studying English is only one side of the coin.

You should also need as much relaxed exposure to English, and as often as you can. And this should be done WITHOUT trying to learn anything. Spend more time **with** English, as if it were your first language. Do things in English often. Remember: a little every day is better than a lot occasionally, because the second you stop doing things in English, you start losing "activation".

So expose yourself to English as much as you can, outside of your study time.

Not just for learning.

But also for relaxation and enjoyment. Watch films in English and forget about trying to learn anything. Read in English and ignore the words you don't know. Spend more time chatting, playing, and just having fun in English. One of the best things I did when I started learning Japanese was change my operating system to Japanese (I have a Mac, so this is easy to do). Every time I use my computer, I'm exposed to Japanese – and I still am.

Passive exposure is practically useless for growing your English. But the goal here is not to grow your English, but rather it is to bring up your overall English activation level.

In Summary

In a nutshell, as I like to say: Focus on chunks and overall meaning, not rules. Don't practise thinking in English, rather, fantasise in English (but keep it natural and real). Lastly, expose yourself to the language as often as you can, and in quantity.

If you do those things consistently and build up the right habits, thinking in English will become second nature. And of course, if you understand WHY you translate and overthink too (which we have talked about extensively in this book), that can only make your life much easier.

It's going to take time, and at first it's going to be hard, and it will be tiring. But do all these things that I've talked about, and the result will be more than worth it, my friend.

AFTERWORD

Thank you again for investing in *Think English, Speak English*, and for choosing to take your journey to speaking amazing, fluent English with me, Dr Julian Northbrook.

I realise for many, this book has been somewhat of a roller-coaster ride, and that I've likely challenged (and hopefully destroyed) many of the beliefs that you had about the way you think about speaking and using English.

The question now, of course, is what you're going to do with the information you've just read?

It's a sad fact that most people will read this book and then never do anything.

From the moment I started teaching, I've been frustrated and disappointed again and again.

It's frustrating for me personally, because writing this book was bloody hard work – just like creating courses and programmes like the ME_FA course and *Extraordinary English Speakers* is super hard work.

Sure, it's nice to get your money in my bank account and ultimately, the sales that come from this book, the courses I make, as well as fees that I get from coaching clients, are what put food on my table, clothes on my kids, and beer in my fridge. The money helps me to live. But more than that, you know what drives me? My "why"? Hearing success stories from people just like you.

Yes, I've heard many over the years.

But I'm a greedy bastard and I want to hear more.

Do me a favour: do the damn work. Implement what you've learned in this book; do something amazing and let me know.

To help you, I've put together a resource that includes some videos and other materials related to what we've talked about in this book. You can find this resource area listed at the very end of this book. My thank you to you for taking the time to read all the way to here.

If you liked this book – or absolutely hated it, either way – do me a favour and review this book on Amazon and/or Good Reads (you can find my profile here: https://www.goodreads.com/author/show/21080345. Julian_Northbrook). There is a section about who I am, if you're interested in that, at the back of the book itself, or you can head on over to https://doingeng-lish.com/about and read the "About" page. Anyway. That about wraps up *Think English, Speak English*. Get the work done and do extraordinary things with your English.

Best,

Dr Julian Northbrook

WHO THE HELL IS DR JULIAN NORTHBROOK?

Hi. I'm Dr Julian Northbrook.

And yes, I am a real doctor.

But please, don't come to me with a heart attack or other medical emergency – I'm not THAT kind of doctor.

More importantly, why should you listen to me?

Well, I could tell you all about my extensive experience teaching and coaching people to speak amazing English, about my master's degree in Applied Linguistics (with distinction, no less) or my Ph.D. research in second-language acquisition, and the publications I have in top academic journals. I *could* tell you all about those things, but I won't, because nobody gives a shit about those qualifications.

What I will tell you about, though, is this – *the pain I experienced while learning my second language.*

You see, there are far, far too many language teachers in the world who have either never learned a second language themselves or have never taken it past the low-intermediate stage.

Should you trust these people?

I say no.

I mean, I certainly wouldn't.

Just like I wouldn't trust a music teacher who couldn't play music, a hairdresser with dirty hair, or a dentist with bad teeth.

In my opinion, the best way to measure a teacher's ability to help you is not by the qualifications they can list, but rather by the number of hours they have spent struggling in a second language themselves.

Well, I've spent *many* hours struggling.

If you want to know more about my story, I've written about it at length here: https://doingenglish.com/about.

But here are some totally random facts about me:

• Dropped out of school at 16 to sleep on my friend's sofa and work in a bacon factory (one of the best "educations" I ever got).

• Got a scholarship to study at an art college where I went to parties every day instead of doing any real work... eventually quit fine art to study fashion design instead.

• After a year of bumming around London, working in a bar in Camden Town, and sleeping on more sofas, I went back to art – this time at university. A lot more parties happened, until one day I suddenly realised it was over and I had nothing to show for my three years at university other than a second-rate degree and a Japanese girlfriend.

• Said *fuck it* to life in the UK and went to Japan for a year in 2007. One year turned into 13 years until I eventually moved to Ireland and got divorced.

• Said I'd learn Japanese after being turned down from the dream job I desperately wanted.

• Got serious about Japanese in 2008 when my then father-in-law told me I had to learn the language if I wanted to marry his daughter (talk about motivation).

• By 2009, I was fairly good enough at Japanese.

• Started work as a freelance translator in 2011, then quit doing it a few months later (I hated translation work).

• Since my idea of being a translator didn't work out, I decided to do a master's degree in Applied Linguistics and English Language Teaching instead via distance learning (which I passed Distinction in half the time I had available – not bad for a school dropout).

• Loved the masters so much I went on to do a Ph.D. in this stuff (studying how "chunks" of English help English learners speak fluently and naturally, and how to design materials in the best possible way to teach these chunks).

• Father of three (very noisy) bilingual children.

• As of February 2020, I'm technically homeless and live permanently in Airbnb's (yes, I picked the worst possible time to start travelling the world).

• Proponent of constant, life-long self-education.

• Avid runner (my best marathon time to date is 3:50:18, at the Los Angeles Marathon 2020).

• Reader (find me on Good Reads).

• Obsessive coffee drinker.

• Fan of '80s synth-pop, techno, and electronic music.

• Very fond of beer, too.

SOME FREE RESOURCES FROM JULIAN

Here are some free resources to further help you on your journey to English mastery.

The Audio version of this book

To get your free audiobook simply scan the following QR code with your phone (or type/ click the URL – but you'll need to do it on your phone, as it doesn't work on desktop).

https://doeng.co/udeSO

Follow the instructions carefully. If it is your first time accessing the Doing English App, you'll need to install it (note: this app isn't available in any of the app stores – **you need to use the link above**).

If you already have the app, the book will simply be added to your existing account.

Important: this audiobook is only available via the app, and you need a smartphone that's not older than my grandfather. If you don't have a smartphone, you can't use this app.

Doing English Daily Newsletter

I write daily English tips emails that you can subscribe to for free. Every day at around 8 am Ireland time, a new email will hit your inbox packed with tips and ideas for speaking better English. This is also the best way to keep up to date with my new books and coaching courses – which I promote in every email.

Sign up here:

https://doingenglish.com/emails

The Rocket Launch Method Training

For a summary of the key points from this book in video format (which lets me visualise some things we talked about here).

Go to:

https://doingenglish.com/freetraining

The Good Shadowing Guide

Shadowing is a great exercise for developing your rhythm, intonation, and "chunking" skills when speaking English – but the way most people do it is wrong. This guide will show you how to use shadowing properly and make it work for you.

You can get it here:

https://doingenglish.com/shadowing

THE IMPLEMENTATION COURSE

After I originally published *Master English FAST* in 2016 (my core book) many people said they wanted more: to go deeper into some topics we discuss, and to get my personal help to customise what they learned in the book, as of course, here in this book. That's why I created the "Master English *FAST* Accelerator" coaching course.

You don't need this course to implement what you've learned here.

But if you want to see the fastest results and transform your English speaking in as little as 90 days, this course may be for you. I've copied the "basic" information page from https://doingenglish.com/mefa below:

————

You can get the basic information quickly, and then if you think the course is right for you... join my free daily emails, and I'll give you more information and then show you how to enrol to the course if you want to.

What is MEFA?

MEFA is a 12-week group coaching course with weekly study and homework tasks designed to:

• Give you as big a boost in English-speaking proficiency, as possible over the 90-day period.

• Get you totally clear about everything you need to do to keep improving with English in your real-life consistently and forever.

Each week's training session, homework task, and the daily feedback from Julian are packed with actionable techniques to change the most important parts of your English as fast as possible.

The weekly group coaching calls and support you get via the discussion group are designed to help you customise what you learn personally.

Requirements

To be right for MEFA, you must meet the following requirements (if you don't meet all of these, there's no point in joining, or even in me sending you more information).

• You must be thick-skinned (I can't work with people who get offended at the slightest criticism).

• You must be able to listen to advice without letting your own (incorrect) opinions about learning English get in the way.

• You must have a real need for English (whether you use English now in work, daily life, or if you have a clear future need – i.e., this is not for hobbyists).

• You must commit to finishing the course. Statistics show the average completion rate for online courses is only between 5% and 15%... the completion rate for MEFA is currently 90%. Why? Because I'm extremely strict about requiring you to submit homework on time, before the deadline. And if you fail to do the work (and don't have a good reason such as an emergency), I will not hide my displeasure.

Also, one more thing:

The MEFA course is not a magic pill that will transform your English simply by joining and doing nothing.

It takes time and work.

For the opportunity to join and for more detailed information about everything we do in MEFA, subscribe to my daily emails:

https://doingenglish.com/emails

OTHER BOOKS BY JULIAN

You can find more low-priced books by Julian Northbrook on Amazon. Go here: https://author.to/JulianNorthbrook

Made in United States
Orlando, FL
07 November 2021

10248780R00048